contents

NZ, Canada, US and UK readers
Please note that Australian cup and spoon
measurements are metric. A quick conversion
guide appears on page 63.

2 ice cold comfort

All the ice-creams in this book are made by freezing in a pan (usually a lamington pan) in the freezer. They have to be beaten twice to prevent ice crystals from forming, but are otherwise easy to make. If you make a lot of ice-cream, however, you might like to invest in an ice-cream maker.

Making ice-cream by hand

Homemade ice-cream, beaten by hand, is usually slightly firmer in texture than ice-cream beaten by machine. This is because an ice-cream churn will incorporate more air than hand beating can do.

Making ice-cream with a churn

There are several different ice-cream churns on the market, some must be churned by turning the handle by hand, others are electrically operated. They continually move the ice-cream mixture around while it's freezing, which produces smooth, creamy ice-cream.

The hand churn is a bucket, usually made of slatted wood, with a metal container inside for the ice-cream mixture. A set of metal blades or paddles rotates inside the container when turned by an external handle. Coarse rock salt and chips of ice are placed between the outside wall of the bucket and the container. This chills the mixture while it is freezing. When the ice-cream is ready, the mixture becomes difficult to churn. A hand-churning ice-cream maker takes a bit of elbow grease, but children love to use it and it does produce excellent ice-cream.

The electric ice-cream churn works in the same way as the hand churn, with salt and ice packed around the metal container. The paddles continuously churn the mixture, only stopping when the mixture becomes too thick for further churning.

Developing time

Ice-creams are at their best if allowed to 'develop' for at least an hour after they have been made. The flavours become stronger and the ice-cream hardens slightly.

Sorbets don't require developing, and can be served as soon as they are made.

Storage
Most homemade ice-creams will keep in the freezer for about one month. Sorbets and frozen yogurts are best eaten within two or three weeks. Store your ice-cream in glass, plastic or metal containers, covered with foil or a lid. Uncovered ice-creams can develop an unpleasant taste.

Texture
Homemade ice-cream freezes to a much harder texture than commercial ice-cream. Take it out of the freezer at least half an hour before serving to soften slightly, otherwise you'll have difficulty scooping it out of the trays.

strawberry
sherbet

500g frozen strawberries

¹/₄ cup (60ml) lemon juice

¹/₄ cup (60ml) water

¹/₄ cup (55g) caster sugar

Blend or process all ingredients until smooth. Pour mixture into lamington pan, cover; freeze about 15 minutes or until firm enough to scoop.

tropical
ice-cream

450g can crushed pineapple in syrup

2 litres (8 cups) vanilla ice-cream, softened

140ml can coconut milk

$^1/_4$ cup (60ml) Midori liqueur

1 tablespoon Malibu rum

$^1/_2$ small (400g) pineapple, sliced

4 medium (340g) kiwi fruit, peeled, sliced

2 medium (300g) carambolas (starfruit), sliced

4 medium (250g) passionfruit, halved

Grease two 8cm x 26cm bar cake pans, line base and 2 long sides with baking paper, extending paper 2cm above edge of pans. Drain canned pineapple well.

Combine ice-cream, milk, canned pineapple, liqueur and rum in large bowl; mix well. Divide evenly between prepared pans. Cover; freeze until ice-cream is firm.

Turn ice-cream out of pans, remove baking paper, cut each into 4 pieces using a serrated knife; cut each piece in half diagonally. Serve with fruit.

Serves 8

6 blueberry
lemon sorbet

500g blueberries

2 cups (500ml) water

1/2 cup (110g) sugar

2 teaspoons finely
grated lemon rind

1/4 cup (60ml) lemon
juice

2 egg whites

Combine blueberries and water in medium pan; simmer, uncovered, 15 minutes. Add sugar, stir over heat, without boiling, until sugar is dissolved. Remove from heat, cool, stir in rind and juice. Blend or process blueberry mixture until smooth. Pour mixture into lamington pan, cover; freeze until sorbet is almost set.

Beat sorbet with egg whites in large bowl with electric mixer, or process, until smooth. Pour into loaf pan, cover; freeze until firm.

Serves 4 to 6

lime and
mint sorbet

You will need about 6 medium (480g) limes for this recipe.

¹/₂ cup (110g) sugar

1¹/₄ cups (310ml) water

1 teaspoon finely grated lime rind

1 cup (250ml) lime juice

2 tablespoons chopped fresh mint leaves

2 egg whites

Combine sugar and water in medium pan, stir over heat, without boiling, until sugar is dissolved. Simmer, uncovered, without stirring, 10 minutes; set aside to cool.

Stir rind, juice and mint into sugar syrup, pour mixture into lamington pan, cover; freeze until almost set.

Beat sorbet with egg whites in large bowl with electric mixer, or process, until smooth. Pour into loaf pan, cover; freeze until firm.

persimmon
ripple
ice-cream

3 medium (900g) persimmons

1²/₃ cups (410ml) thickened cream

1¹/₄ cups (310ml) milk

¹/₄ cup (60ml) honey

6 egg yolks

¹/₄ cup (55g) caster sugar

Line the base and sides of 14cm x 21cm loaf pan with baking paper.

Peel persimmons; process flesh until smooth. Bring cream, milk and honey to boil in medium pan. Beat egg yolks and sugar in medium bowl with electric mixer until creamy, gradually whisk into hot cream mixture. Stir over heat, without boiling, until mixture thickens slightly; remove from heat. Strain custard into lamington pan. Cover; freeze until almost set.

Chop ice-cream roughly, beat in large bowl with electric mixer, or process, until smooth. Pour half the ice-cream into prepared pan, swirl in ¹/₄ cup (60ml) persimmon puree. Pour in remaining ice-cream mixture, swirl in another ¹/₄ cup (60ml) persimmon puree, cover; freeze until firm.

Turn ice-cream onto board, peel away paper, slice ice-cream and serve with remaining persimmon puree.

Serves 6

10 kiwi fruit
water ice

8 (680g) kiwi fruit,
peeled, chopped
roughly

1 cup (220g) sugar

1 cup (250ml) water

1 cup (250ml) dry
white wine

1 cup (250ml) water,
extra

Blend or process kiwi fruit until smooth, push mixture through fine sieve;
discard seeds.

Combine sugar and water in medium pan, stir over heat, without boiling,
until sugar is dissolved. Boil, uncovered, 3 minutes, remove from heat;
cool 10 minutes. Stir kiwi fruit puree and remaining ingredients into syrup.
Pour mixture into lamington pan, cover; freeze until mixture is starting to
set around edges of pan.

Mix well, using a fork. Spoon into loaf pan, cover; freeze until firm.

vanilla
ice-cream

³/₄ *cup (165g) sugar*

4cm piece vanilla bean, split lengthways

600ml thickened cream

Combine sugar, vanilla bean and half the cream in medium pan, stir over heat, without boiling, until sugar is dissolved. Remove from heat, stir in remaining cream; discard vanilla bean. Strain mixture through fine cloth into lamington pan, cover; freeze until just set.

Chop ice-cream roughly, beat in large bowl with electric mixer, or process, until smooth. Pour into lamington pan; freeze again, repeat beating process once more. Pour into loaf pan, cover; freeze until firm.

12 chocolate hazelnut ice-cream

2 litres (8 cups) vanilla ice-cream

³/₄ cup (180ml) chocolate hazelnut spread, warmed

¹/₂ cup (60g) chopped roasted hazelnuts

1 tablespoon Kahlua

2 teaspoons dry instant coffee

Line 14cm x 21cm loaf pan with strip of baking paper to cover base and extend over 2 opposite sides.

Divide ice-cream in half, return 1 half to freezer.

Beat softened ice-cream with chocolate hazelnut spread in small bowl with electric mixer until smooth; stir in nuts. Pour mixture into prepared pan, cover; freeze until firm. Combine liqueur and coffee in bowl, stir until coffee is dissolved. Beat remaining softened ice-cream in small bowl with electric mixer until smooth. Stir in liqueur mixture. Pour over ice-cream in pan, cover; freeze until firm. Turn ice-cream onto board, remove paper; serve sliced.

Serves 6 to 8

citus gelato

1 cup (220g) sugar

1 cup (250ml) dry
white wine

1 cup (250ml) water

1/2 cup (125ml) orange
juice

1/4 cup (60ml) lime
juice

1/4 cup (60ml) lemon
juice

2 egg whites

Combine sugar, wine and water in medium pan, stir over heat, without
boiling, until sugar is dissolved. Simmer, uncovered, about 10 minutes or
until reduced to 1¹/2 cups (375ml).

Stir strained juices into cooled syrup. Pour mixture into lamington pan,
cover; freeze until almost set.

Beat gelato with egg whites in large bowl with electric mixer, or process,
until smooth. Return to lamington pan, cover; freeze until almost set. Beat
or process mixture again, pour into loaf pan, cover; freeze until firm,

Serves 6

14 lime and pear
ice-cream
with poached pears

You will need about 4 medium (320g) limes for this recipe.

1 cup (250ml) milk

5 egg yolks

1/2 cup (110g) caster sugar

2 medium pears (460g), peeled, chopped

1/3 cup (80ml) lime juice

300ml thickened cream

poached pears

2 medium pears (460g)

1/4 cup (60ml) water

1/4 cup (60m) lime juice

1 tablespoon sugar

Cover the base and sides of a 14cm x 21cm loaf pan with foil.

Bring milk to boil in medium pan. Beat egg yolks and sugar in small bowl with electric mixer until thick and creamy, gradually whisk egg mixture into hot milk, whisk over heat, without boiling, until mixture thickens slightly. Transfer mixture to large bowl; beat with electric mixer about 15 minutes or until thick.

Blend or process pears and juice until smooth; fold into custard mixture. Beat cream in small bowl with electric mixer until soft peaks form, fold into pear mixture. Pour mixture into prepared pan. Cover; freeze until firm. Turn ice-cream onto board, remove foil; serve sliced with Poached Pears.

Poached Pears Peel, quarter, core and slice pears. Combine water, juice and sugar in medium pan, bring to boil. Add pears; simmer, covered, about 5 minutes or until just tender, cool.

Serves 6

16 lime pistachio
sherbet

You will need about 8 medium limes (640g) for this recipe.

1 cup (220g) sugar

2¹/₂ cups (625ml) water

2 teaspoons finely grated lime rind

1¹/₄ cups (310ml) lime juice

¹/₄ cup (35g) pistachios, chopped finely

2 egg whites

green food colouring, optional

Combine sugar and water in medium pan, stir over heat, without boiling, until sugar is dissolved. Simmer, uncovered, without stirring, about 10 minutes or until mixture is thickened slightly; cool. Stir rind, juice and nuts into sugar syrup. Pour mixture into lamington pan, cover; freeze until almost set.

Beat sherbet, egg whites and a little colouring in large bowl with electric mixer, until smooth. Pour into loaf pan, cover; freeze until firm.

Serves 4 to 6

frozen
christmas pudding
with butterscotch sauce

600ml thickened cream

1/2 cup (80g) icing sugar mixture

1 tablespoon dark rum

2 1/2 cups (500g) bottled fruit mince

butterscotch sauce

3/4 cup (150g) firmly packed brown sugar

3/4 cup (180ml) thickened cream

185g butter, chopped

Beat cream and sifted icing sugar in large bowl with electric mixer until firm peaks form. Gently fold in the rum and fruit mince.

Pour mixture into 1.5-litre (6-cup) aluminium pudding steamer, tap gently on bench to remove air bubbles. Cover; freeze until firm.

To serve, dip base of steamer in hot water, turn onto dish. Serve with warm Butterscotch Sauce.

Butterscotch Sauce Combine all ingredients in medium pan, stir over heat, without boiling, until sugar is dissolved. Simmer, uncovered, stirring, 3 minutes.

Serves 6 to 8

18 prickly pear
sorbet

Use rubber gloves while peeling and chopping prickly pears.

8 pink prickly pears (870g), peeled, chopped

3/4 cup (165g) sugar

2 cups (500ml) water

1/4 cup (60ml) orange juice

4 egg whites

Blend or process prickly pears until smooth, push through coarse sieve; discard seeds and pulp. Combine sugar and water in medium pan, stir over heat, without boiling, until sugar is dissolved. Simmer, uncovered, without stirring, 15 minutes; cool.

Stir pear puree and orange juice into sugar syrup, pour mixture into lamington pan, cover; freeze until almost set.

Beat sorbet with egg whites in large bowl with electric mixer, or process, until smooth. Pour into loaf pan, cover; freeze until firm.

Serves 6

mango
ice-cream

You will need about 4 medium (1.7kg) mangoes for this recipe.

1 tablespoon gelatine

$^1/_4$ cup (60ml) water

3 cups (600g) chopped mango

$^3/_4$ cup (165g) caster sugar

1 tablespoon orange juice

300ml thickened cream

Soften gelatine in water in cup, stir over simmering water until dissolved. Pour gelatine mixture into bowl, stir in mango, sugar and orange juice, stir until sugar is dissolved. Place mixture in lamington pan, cover; freeze until almost set.

Chop ice-cream roughly, process until pale in colour. Beat cream in small bowl with electric mixer until soft peaks form, fold into mango mixture.

Pour into loaf pan, cover; freeze until firm. Remove from freezer 15 minutes before serving.

frozen

apricot amaretto parfait

1/3 cup (80ml) water

1 cup (220g) sugar

8 egg yolks

1 cup (250ml) thickened cream

3/4 cup (185g) mascarpone cheese

1/4 cup (60ml) Amaretto liqueur

100g chopped chocolate honeycomb pieces

1/2 cup (80g) chopped almond kernels, toasted

5 large (400g) apricots, seeded, sliced

toffee curls

1/4 cup (55g) caster sugar

Grease 14cm x 21cm loaf pan, cover base and sides with plastic wrap, extending enough wrap over sides to completely cover top of pan.

Combine water and sugar in small pan, stir over heat, without boiling, until sugar is dissolved. Simmer, uncovered, without stirring, about 5 minutes or until mixture is thickened slightly. Beat egg yolks in small bowl with electric mixer until thick and creamy. Gradually pour in hot syrup, in a thin stream; continue beating about 10 minutes or until cool.

Transfer egg mixture to large bowl. Beat cream in small bowl with electric mixer until soft peaks form, stir in cheese and liqueur, then fold in remaining ingredients. Fold into egg mixture, pour into prepared pan, cover; freeze until firm.

Turn parfait onto board, remove plastic wrap, cut into 8 slices, then halve each on the diagonal. Serve with Toffee Curls.

Toffee Curls Cover back of oven tray with foil, lightly grease foil, sprinkle half the sugar randomly over foil, place under hot grill until sugar is melted and light brown.

Stand toffee about 30 seconds; while it is still warm, peel it away from the foil in strips, curling and shaping the toffee as you remove it. Cool. Repeat process, re-greasing foil, using remaining sugar.

Serves 8

22 plum ice-cream

6 medium (675g) blood plums

2 cups (500ml) milk

1 cup (250ml) cream

1 vanilla bean

6 egg yolks

1/2 cup (110g) caster sugar

2 tablespoons custard powder

300ml cream, extra

Cut a small cross on base of plums, place in large pan of boiling water, return to boil; drain. Place plums in large bowl of cold water, stand 5 minutes; drain. Peel away and discard skins, chop plums coarsely.

Heat milk, cream and split bean in medium pan; remove bean. Whisk egg yolks, sugar and custard powder in small bowl until combined; whisk into milk mixture. Whisk over heat, without boiling, until mixture thickens, cover surface of custard with plastic wrap; cool.

Stir plums and extra cream into custard, pour into lamington pan. Cover; freeze until almost set.

Chop ice-cream roughly, beat in large bowl with electric mixer, or process, until smooth. Pour into loaf pan, cover; freeze until firm.

Serves 6

lychee, ginger and lime ice

425g can lychees in syrup

2¹/₂ cups (625ml) water

1¹/₂ cups (330g) sugar

1 teaspoon finely grated fresh ginger

1 large orange (300g), segmented

1 teaspoon finely grated lime rind

¹/₄ cup (60ml) lime juice

Drain lychees, reserve syrup. Combine water, sugar and reserved syrup in medium pan, stir over heat, without boiling, until sugar is dissolved. Stir in ginger; boil, uncovered, 5 minutes.

Chop orange segments, stir into lychee syrup with rind and juice; simmer, uncovered, 3 minutes, cool. Pour mixture into lamington pan, cover; freeze until almost set.

Mix well, using a fork. Spoon into loaf pan, cover; freeze until firm. Serve with lychees.

Serves 6

caramel
macadamia
ice-cream

4 x 60g Snickers bars,
chopped

*1/2 cup (125ml)
thickened cream*

*1 litre (4 cups)
caramel ice-cream*

*1 cup (150g)
macadamias, toasted,
chopped*

Place a collar of baking paper or foil around 4 x 3/4-cup (180ml)
freezerproof dishes; secure with rubber band.

Combine Snickers and cream in medium heavy-based pan, stir over low
heat until Snickers are melted; cool. Beat softened ice-cream in large bowl
with electric mixer until smooth. Add Snickers mixture and 3/4 cup (110g)
of the nuts, stir until combined. Divide mixture among prepared dishes,
cover; freeze until firm. Remove collars, press remaining nuts on side of
ice-cream.

chocolate and cinnamon
ice-cream

2 cups (500ml) milk

3 cinnamon sticks, halved

170g bittersweet chocolate, chopped finely

8 egg yolks

$1/2$ cup (110g) caster sugar

300ml thickened cream

Place milk, cinnamon and chocolate in large heavy-based pan, stir over low heat until chocolate is melted. Remove from heat, stand 5 minutes, strain into jug; discard cinnamon sticks.

Beat egg yolks and sugar in small bowl with electric mixer until thick and creamy. Gradually add hot chocolate mixture to egg yolk mixture, beating until just combined. Return mixture to same pan, stir over heat, without boiling, about 15 minutes or until mixture thickens slightly. Remove from heat, transfer to large bowl, cover surface of custard with plastic wrap; cool. Refrigerate about 1 hour or until mixture is cold.

Stir in cream, then pour into lamington pan, cover; freeze until just set.
Chop ice-cream roughly, beat in large bowl with electric mixer, or process, until smooth. Pour into loaf pan, cover; freeze until firm.

Serves 6

26 chocolate honeycomb ice-cream towers

2 cups (500ml) milk

300ml cream

5 egg yolks

$^{1}/_{2}$ cup (110g) caster sugar

1 tablespoon custard powder

100g dark cooking chocolate, chopped finely

$^{1}/_{4}$ cup (60ml) Kahlua liqueur

50g chocolate honeycomb bars, chopped coarsely

1$^{1}/_{3}$ cups (200g) dark chocolate Melts, melted

Grease 6 x $^{3}/_{4}$-cup (180ml) dishes, line with plastic wrap, bringing wrap 5cm over sides. Freeze until ready to use.

Combine milk and cream in medium pan, bring to boil. Whisk egg yolks, sugar and custard powder in medium bowl until combined, gradually whisk in hot milk mixture. Add dark chocolate, stir until melted, stir in liqueur. Pour mixture into lamington pan, cover; freeze until ice-cream is almost set.

Chop ice-cream roughly, beat in large bowl with electric mixer, or process, until smooth. Reserve 1 tablespoon of the chopped honeycomb; stir remaining chocolate honeycomb into ice-cream. Spoon ice-cream into prepared dishes, smooth top, tap gently on bench to remove air bubbles. Enclose dishes in plastic wrap; freeze until firm.

Finely chop reserved chocolate honeycomb. Spread melted chocolate evenly over 2 sheets of baking paper, each about 26cm x 28cm, sprinkle reserved honeycomb evenly over chocolate, leave to set.

Carefully remove chocolate from paper, break into long wedges, about 3cm x 13cm each.

Turn ice-cream onto plates, remove wrap, gently press chocolate wedges around sides. Serve immediately.

Serves 6

easy fruity
ice-cream

1 medium (200g)
banana, chopped

2 tablespoons lemon
juice

375ml can evaporated
milk, chilled

3/4 cup (165g) caster
sugar

1 medium (240g)
orange, chopped

Combine banana and
juice in small bowl.
Beat milk in medium
bowl with electric
mixer until thick and
fluffy, gradually beat
in sugar, beating until
dissolved between
additions. Stir in
banana mixture and
orange, pour into loaf
pan, cover; freeze
until firm. Serve with
passionfruit and extra
orange, if desired.

Serves 4

rocky road

ice-cream

with hot fudge sauce

2 litres (8 cups) vanilla ice-cream

100g dark cooking chocolate, chopped

1/2 cup (45g) coconut, toasted

1/2 cup (75g) peanuts, toasted, chopped

100g packet fruity Mallow Bakes

hot fudge sauce
300ml cream

100g packet white marshmallows

200g dark cooking chocolate, chopped

Line base and sides of 14cm x 21cm loaf pan with baking paper. Combine 1/2 cup (125ml) of the softened ice-cream with chocolate in medium heatproof bowl, stir over pan of simmering water until melted. Remove from heat, stand 10 minutes.

Combine remaining softened ice-cream with remaining ingredients in large bowl; swirl chocolate mixture through ice-cream mixture. Pour into prepared pan, cover; freeze until firm. Turn ice-cream onto plate, remove paper; serve sliced with Hot Fudge Sauce.

Hot Fudge Sauce Combine all ingredients in medium pan, stir over low heat, without boiling, until marshmallows and chocolate are melted.

Serves 8

30 orange and mango ice

1/2 cup (110g) sugar

1/2 cup (125ml) water

1/4 cup (60ml) dry white wine

2 medium mangoes (860g), peeled, chopped

2 cups (500ml) orange juice

2 egg whites

Combine sugar, water and wine in medium pan, stir over heat, without boiling, until sugar is dissolved. Simmer, uncovered, without stirring, 10 minutes; cool.

Blend or process mango and juice until smooth, stir into sugar syrup. Pour mixture into lamington pan, cover; freeze until almost set.

Beat mixture with egg whites in large bowl with electric mixer, or process, until smooth. Pour into loaf pan, cover; freeze until firm.

pumpkin and maple ice-cream

You will need to cook about 300g pumpkin for this recipe.

6 egg yolks

¹/₃ cup (75g) caster sugar

¹/₃ cup (80ml) maple syrup

³/₄ cup cooked mashed pumpkin

300ml thickened cream

¹/₂ teaspoon ground nutmeg

Beat egg yolks and sugar in small bowl with electric mixer until thick and creamy, gradually beat in syrup, then pumpkin. Transfer mixture to large bowl. Beat cream and nutmeg in small bowl with electric mixer until soft peaks form, fold into pumpkin mixture. Pour mixture into lamington pan, cover; freeze until almost set.
Chop ice-cream roughly, beat in large bowl with electric mixer, or process, until smooth. Pour into loaf pan, cover; freeze until firm.

32 the essential crunch

To offset the smooth creaminess of ice-creams and sorbets, you need a sweet crisp biscuit. Here are four of the world's favourite ice-cream accompaniments.

pistachio biscotti

2 cups (300g) plain flour

3 eggs, lightly beaten

1 cup (220g) caster sugar

1/2 teaspoon grated orange rind

1/2 teaspoon vanilla essence

1/4 teaspoon baking powder

2/3 cup (100g) shelled pistachios, toasted

Sift flour into bowl, add eggs, sugar, rind, essence and baking powder, mix to a smooth dough; mix in nuts.
Divide dough in half, roll each half on lightly floured surface to a 20cm sausage shape; place on greased oven tray. Bake in moderate oven about 30 minutes or until lightly browned and crusty; cool on trays.
Cut diagonally into 1.5cm slices, using a serrated knife. Place slices, cut side up, on greased oven trays. Bake in moderate oven about 25 minutes or until crisp; cool on wire racks.

Makes about 26

brandy snaps

60g butter

1/3 cup (75g) brown sugar

2 tablespoons golden syrup

1/2 teaspoon ground ginger

1/2 cup (75g) plain flour

1/2 teaspoon lemon juice

Combine butter, sugar, golden syrup and ginger in small pan, stir over heat, without boiling, until butter is melted. Remove from heat, stir in flour and juice.
Drop level tablespoons of mixture about 6cm apart on greased oven trays. Bake in moderate oven about 7 minutes or until snaps are bubbling and golden brown; remove from oven.
Slide a spatula under each snap, then wrap quickly around the handle of a wooden spoon. Remove spoon handle, then place snaps on wire rack to cool and become firm. Repeat with the remaining mixture.

Makes about 10

langues de chat
(cat's tongues)

60g butter

1/2 cup (110g) caster sugar

2 egg whites, beaten lightly

1/2 cup (50g) plain flour

Beat butter and sugar in small bowl with electric mixer until smooth. Stir in egg whites and flour. Spoon mixture into piping bag fitted with 5mm plain tube. Pipe 8cm-long strips, (making them slightly wider at each end) about 4cm apart on greased oven trays, allow about 6 per tray. Tap tray firmly on bench to spread mixture slightly.

Bake in hot oven about 4 minutes or until edges are lightly browned; cool on wire racks.

Makes about 24

almond tuiles

1 egg white

1/4 cup (55g) caster sugar

1/4 cup (40g) plain flour

1/2 teaspoon vanilla essence

2 tablespoons flaked almonds

30g butter, melted

Combine all ingredients in small bowl; mix well.

Drop 1 1/2 level teaspoons of mixture about 6cm apart on greased oven trays. For easy handling it is best to bake only 3 tuiles at a time. Spread mixture into circles with the back of a teaspoon.

Bake in moderate oven for about 5 minutes or until tuiles brown around the edges. Remove from tray with a spatula and place over a rolling pin to cool and curl.

Makes about 35

From left: almond tuiles, brandy snaps, pistachio biscotti, langues de chat.

tutti-frutti
pops

*You will need about
4 passionfruit for this
recipe.*

*1 litre (4 cups) vanilla
ice-cream*

*500g (2 cups) mango
frozen yogurt*

*440g can mango
slices, drained,
chopped*

*1/3 cup (80ml)
passionfruit pulp*

*16 wooden hobby
sticks*

Beat softened ice-
cream and yogurt
in large bowl with
electric mixer until
smooth, stir in mango
and passionfruit.
Divide mixture among
16 x 100ml ice-block
moulds, insert hobby
sticks in centre of
each; freeze until firm.

Serves 16

peachy milk
ice

825g can peach halves in natural juice, drained

2 x 375ml cans evaporated light milk

¼ cup (55g) caster sugar

Blend or process peaches until smooth, combine with milk in large bowl, stir in sugar. Pour mixture into lamington pan, cover; freeze until almost set.

Beat mixture in large bowl with electric mixer, or process, until smooth. Pour into loaf pan, cover; freeze until firm. Remove from freezer 10 minutes before serving.

Serves 6

lime
ice-cream

You will need about 2 medium (160g) limes for this recipe.

1 teaspoon finely grated lime rind

⅓ cup (80ml) lime juice

3 eggs, beaten lightly

¼ cup (55g) caster sugar

300ml thickened cream

green food colouring, optional

Bring rind and juice to boil in small pan; simmer, uncovered, until reduced by half, cool.

Beat eggs and sugar in medium heatproof bowl, with electric mixer, over pan of simmering water, about 10 minutes or until thick and creamy, cover surface with plastic wrap; cool.

Stir lime mixture into egg mixture. Beat cream in small bowl with electric mixer until soft peaks form, fold into egg mixture, tint with colouring, if desired. Pour mixture into lamington pan, cover; freeze until almost set.

Chop ice-cream roughly, beat in large bowl with electric mixer, or process, until smooth. Pour into loaf pan, cover; freeze until firm.

apricot
ice-cream
with chocolate coconut sauce

$^3/_4$ cup (110g) dried apricots
$^1/_2$ cup (125ml) water
2 tablespoons sugar
$^1/_4$ cup (55g) sugar, extra
$^1/_3$ cup (80ml) water, extra
3 egg yolks
300ml thickened cream

chocolate coconut sauce
60g dark chocolate Melts
$^1/_2$ cup (125ml) cream
$^1/_4$ cup (20g) desiccated coconut

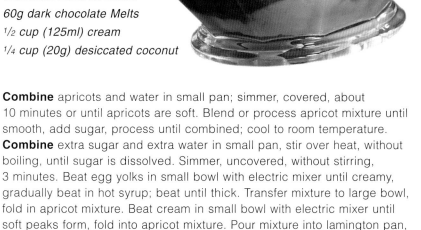

Combine apricots and water in small pan; simmer, covered, about
10 minutes or until apricots are soft. Blend or process apricot mixture until
smooth, add sugar, process until combined; cool to room temperature.
Combine extra sugar and extra water in small pan, stir over heat, without
boiling, until sugar is dissolved. Simmer, uncovered, without stirring,
3 minutes. Beat egg yolks in small bowl with electric mixer until creamy,
gradually beat in hot syrup; beat until thick. Transfer mixture to large bowl,
fold in apricot mixture. Beat cream in small bowl with electric mixer until
soft peaks form, fold into apricot mixture. Pour mixture into lamington pan,
cover; freeze until almost set.
Chop ice-cream roughly, beat in large bowl with electric mixer, or process,
until smooth. Pour into loaf pan, cover; freeze until firm. Serve with warm
Chocolate Coconut Sauce.
Chocolate Coconut Sauce Combine all ingredients in small pan, stir over
heat, without boiling, until pouring consistency.

38

licorice
ice-cream

3 x 50g packets
licorice toffees

1 cup (250ml) milk

300ml thickened
cream

2 tablespoons caster
sugar

4 egg yolks

Combine toffees, milk and cream in medium pan, stir over heat, without
boiling, until toffees have dissolved. Bring to boil, remove from heat.
Beat sugar and egg yolks in small bowl with electric mixer until thick and
creamy. Whisk hot milk mixture into egg yolk mixture in bowl. Pour mixture
into lamington pan, cover; freeze until almost set.
Chop ice-cream roughly, beat in large bowl with electric mixer, or process,
until smooth. Pour into loaf pan, cover; freeze until firm.

Serves 6

melon
sorbet

Use melons of your choice.

½ cup (110g) sugar

1 cup (250ml) water

400g melon flesh

2 egg whites

Combine sugar and water in medium pan, stir over heat, without boiling, until sugar is dissolved. Simmer, uncovered, without stirring, 10 minutes; cool. Blend or process the melon until smooth; you will need 2 cups (500ml) puree.

Stir melon puree into sugar syrup, pour into lamington pan, cover; freeze until almost set.

Beat sorbet with egg whites in large bowl with electric mixer, or process, until smooth. Pour into loaf pan, cover; freeze until firm.

40 mango ginger
sorbet

1¹/₂ cups (375ml) water

¹/₄ cup (55g) sugar

2 small (600g) mangoes

2 tablespoons lemon juice

2 teaspoons chopped glace ginger

2 egg whites

Combine water and sugar in medium pan, stir over heat, without boiling, until sugar is dissolved. Boil, uncovered, without stirring, about 5 minutes or until thickened slightly, cool. Refrigerate syrup until cold.

Process mango flesh, juice, ginger and syrup until smooth. Pour mixture into lamington pan, cover; freeze until almost set.

Beat sorbet with egg whites in large bowl with electric mixer, or process, until smooth. Pour into loaf pan, cover; freeze until firm.

avocado
ice-cream

2 large (640g) ripe avocados

1¹/₂ cups (375ml) thickened cream

1 cup (250ml) coconut cream

¹/₂ cup (125ml) maple syrup

¹/₄ cup (40g) icing sugar mixture

1 tablespoon finely grated lemon rind

2 tablespoons lemon juice

Process avocados until smooth, add remaining ingredients, process until combined. Spoon mixture into plastic wrap-lined lamington pan, cover; freeze until almost set.

Chop ice-cream roughly, beat in large bowl with electric mixer, or process, until smooth. Spoon into plastic wrap-lined loaf pan, cover; freeze until firm. Remove ice-cream from freezer 15 minutes before serving to allow to soften slightly.

Serves 6

42

tiramisu
ice-cream
with liqueur berries

1¹/₂ cups (375ml) milk

8 egg yolks

¹/₂ cup (110g) caster sugar

2¹/₂ tablespoons dry instant coffee

¹/₂ cup (125ml) hot milk, extra

10 sponge finger biscuits

1 cup (250g) mascarpone cheese

¹/₃ cup (80ml) thickened cream

¹/₄ cup (60ml) Kahlua

100g finely chopped dark chocolate

liqueur berries

500g strawberries, halved

300g blueberries

¹/₃ cup (80ml) Kahlua liqueur

1 tablespoon caster sugar

200g raspberries

Bring milk to boil in large heavy-based pan, remove from heat. Whisk egg yolks and sugar in large bowl with electric mixer until thick and creamy.

Gradually whisk in hot milk, return to same pan, stir over low heat, without boiling, until mixture thickens slightly. Transfer custard to large bowl, cover surface with plastic wrap; refrigerate until cold.

Dissolve coffee in extra milk. Place biscuits in single layer, in large shallow dish, pour coffee mixture over biscuits, stand until liquid is absorbed; chop biscuits.

Whisk the mascarpone into custard, stir in remaining ingredients and biscuits. Pour mixture into lamington pan, cover; freeze until just set.

Chop ice-cream roughly, beat in large bowl with electric mixer until almost smooth. Pour into loaf pan, cover; freeze until firm. Serve ice-cream with Liqueur Berries.

Liqueur Berries Combine all ingredients, except raspberries, in large bowl, cover; refrigerate 3 hours or overnight. Just before serving, gently stir in raspberries.

Serves 6 to 8

44 passionfruit
ice-cream

You will need about 8 passionfruit for this recipe.

2 cups (500ml) milk

8 egg yolks

$^2/_3$ cup (150g) caster sugar

$^2/_3$ cup (160ml) passionfruit pulp

300ml thickened cream

Bring milk to boil in medium pan. Whisk egg yolks and sugar in medium bowl until creamy, gradually whisk into hot milk, stir over heat, without boiling, until mixture thickens slightly, cover surface of custard with plastic wrap; cool. Refrigerate 1 hour or until cold.

Stir passionfruit and cream into custard. Pour mixture into lamington pan, cover; freeze until almost set.

Chop ice-cream roughly, beat in large bowl with electric mixer, until smooth. Pour into loaf pan, cover; freeze until firm.

Serves 4 to 6

cassata

1 litre (4 cups)
chocolate ice-cream

100g dark cooking
chocolate, chopped
finely

2 litres (8 cups) vanilla
ice-cream

2 tablespoons
chopped red glace
cherries

2 tablespoons
chopped green glace
cherries

1/3 cup (85g) glace
apricots, chopped
finely

1 tablespoon Kahlua
liqueur

1/3 cup (25g) flaked
almonds, toasted

1/4 teaspoon almond
essence

cocoa powder optional

Grease a deep 20cm round cake pan, line base
and side with baking paper. Combine softened
chocolate ice-cream with chocolate in medium
bowl, spread into prepared pan, cover; freeze.
Combine half the softened vanilla ice-cream
with cherries, apricots and liqueur, spread over
chocolate ice-cream, cover; freeze until firm.
Combine remaining softened vanilla ice-cream
with almonds and essence; spread over fruit
ice-cream.
Smooth top, cover; freeze until firm. Turn
ice-cream onto plate, remove paper; sift cocoa
powder over top if desired. Stand 10 minutes
before serving.

Serves 8

chocolate
cookie
ice-cream

*2 litres (8 cups) vanilla
ice-cream*

*200g packet Tim Tam
biscuits, chopped
coarsely*

*200ml bottle chocolate
Ice Magic*

6 ice-cream cones

Beat softened ice-cream in large bowl with electric mixer until smooth, stir in biscuits. Drizzle 1/2 cup (125ml) of Ice Magic over surface of ice-cream, stand until set; stir to break up pieces. Pour into loaf pan, cover; freeze until firm.

Scoop out ice-cream, serve in cones; drizzle scoops with remaining Ice Magic.

Serves 6

honey
ice-cream

3 eggs

3 egg yolks

¹/₂ cup (125ml) honey

600ml thickened cream

Combine eggs, egg yolks and honey in medium heatproof bowl, whisk over pan of simmering water about 10 minutes or until mixture is thick and creamy. Remove from heat, stir in half the cream. Pour mixture into lamington pan, cover; freeze until just set.

Chop ice-cream roughly, beat in large bowl with electric mixer, or process, until smooth. Beat remaining cream in small bowl with electric mixer until soft peaks form, gently fold into ice-cream mixture. Pour into loaf pan, cover; freeze until firm.

Serves 4 to 6

white chocolate and strawberry bombe

¹/₂ cup (110g) caster sugar

2 tablespoons dry instant coffee

1¹/₂ cups (375ml) water

250g packet sponge finger biscuits

3 eggs, separated

1 cup (250g) mascarpone cheese

¹/₂ cup (110g) caster sugar, extra

¹/₂ cup (125ml) thickened cream

125g white chocolate, chopped finely

375g strawberries, sliced

Combine sugar, coffee and water in small pan, stir over low heat, without boiling, until sugar is dissolved. Immerse ³/₄ of the biscuits, 1 at a time, in coffee mixture, then arrange them, in single layer, over base and side of a 2-litre (8-cup) aluminium pudding steamer.

Beat egg whites in small bowl with electric mixer until firm peaks form.

Beat egg yolks, mascarpone, extra sugar and cream in medium bowl with electric mixer until smooth; fold in egg whites and chocolate. Spread half the cream mixture over biscuits in steamer, top with half the strawberries; repeat layers.

Dip remaining biscuits in remaining coffee mixture; arrange over strawberries. Cover; freeze until firm. Turn onto plate about 10 minutes before serving.

Serves 8 to 10

watermelon
ice

1.5kg watermelon

1 cup (250ml) water

2/3 cup (150g) sugar

2 tablespoons orange juice

1 egg white

Remove rind from watermelon, chop flesh. Blend or process watermelon flesh until just smooth; strain through coarse sieve to remove seeds. You will need 3¹/₂ cups (875ml) watermelon puree.

Combine watermelon puree, water, sugar and juice in large pan, stir over low heat, without boiling, until sugar is dissolved. Simmer, uncovered, 5 minutes; cool.

Pour mixture into lamington pan, cover; freeze until almost set.

Beat mixture with egg white in large bowl with electric mixer, or process, until smooth. Pour into loaf pan, cover; freeze until firm.

1 medium kumara (400g), peeled, chopped finely

2 cups (500ml) milk

1/4 cup (55g) sugar

1 1/2 teaspoons ground cardamom

400g can sweetened condensed milk

300ml thickened cream

Combine kumara, milk, sugar and cardamom in medium pan, stir over heat, without boiling, until sugar is dissolved. Simmer, covered, about 15 minutes or until kumara is tender; cool. Blend or process kumara mixture, in batches, until smooth, stir in condensed milk. Pour mixture into lamington pan, cover; freeze until almost set.

Chop ice-cream roughly, beat with cream, in large bowl with electric mixer, or process, until smooth. Pour into loaf pan, cover; freeze until firm.

Serves 6

52 strawberry
ice-cream cake

280g packet golden sponge cake mix (plus ingredients listed on packet)

$^1/_4$ cup (60ml) Cointreau

strawberry ice-cream

250g strawberries

2 litres (8 cups) vanilla ice-cream

2 teaspoons finely grated orange rind

red food colouring, optional

Grease a deep 22cm round cake pan, line the base and side with baking paper.

Make cake mix according to packet directions. Spread into prepared pan, bake in moderate oven about 30 minutes. Turn cake onto wire rack to cool. Split cold cake in half horizontally.

Line base and side of deep 22cm round cake pan with plastic wrap.

Place bottom layer of cake in base of pan, brush with half the liqueur, top with Strawberry Ice-cream. Brush remaining cake layer with remaining liqueur, place over ice-cream, cut side down. Cover; freeze until firm.

Remove from freezer 10 minutes before serving.

Strawberry Ice-Cream Blend or process strawberries until smooth. Combine softened ice-cream with strawberry puree, rind and a few drops of food colouring in large bowl; stir until just combined.

Serves 6 to 8

coffee
amaretti ice-cream

6 egg yolks

600ml thickened cream

1^1/$_2$ cups (375ml) milk

1 cup (200g) firmly packed brown sugar

2 teaspoons dry instant coffee

10 (60g) amaretti biscuits, crushed finely

^{1}/$_3$ cup (35g) grated dark chocolate

Combine egg yolks, cream, milk, sugar and coffee in medium pan, stir over low heat, without boiling, until mixture thickens slightly. Cover surface of custard with plastic wrap, cool. Pour into lamington pan, cover; freeze until almost set.

Chop ice-cream roughly, beat in large bowl with electric mixer, or process, until smooth. Stir in crushed biscuits and chocolate. Pour into loaf pan, cover; freeze until firm.

Serves 6

nesselrode
ice-cream

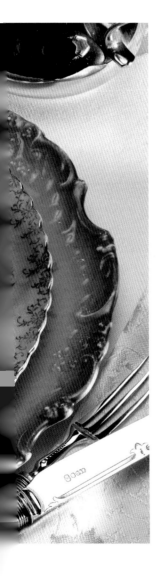

¹/₃ cup (85g) finely chopped glace apricots

2 tablespoons brandy

300ml thickened cream

4 eggs, separated

¹/₂ cup (80g) icing sugar

250g can sweetened chestnut spread

toasted flaked almonds

apricot sauce

1 cup (150g) finely chopped dried apricots

1 cup (250ml) water

1¹/₄ cups (310ml) orange juice

Line a 14cm x 21cm loaf pan with plastic wrap.

Combine apricots and brandy in small bowl; stand 20 minutes. Beat cream in small bowl with electric mixer until soft peaks form.

Beat egg whites in small bowl with electric mixer until soft peaks form. Add sifted icing sugar gradually, beat until dissolved. Transfer mixture to large bowl; fold in cream, egg yolks, apricot mixture and chestnut spread. Pour mixture into prepared pan, cover; freeze until firm.

Turn ice-cream onto board, remove plastic wrap, serve sliced with Apricot Sauce and flaked almonds.

Apricot Sauce Combine apricots and water in small pan; simmer, covered, about 10 minutes or until apricots are soft, cool. Blend or process apricot mixture and juice until smooth; strain.

Serves 8

mulled wine
sorbet

¹/₂ cup (110g) sugar

1¹/₄ cups (310ml) water

1¹/₂ cups (375ml) dry red wine

¹/₄ cup (60ml) orange juice

2 tablespoons redcurrant jelly

1 cinnamon stick

5 whole cloves

¹/₄ teaspoon ground nutmeg

1 egg white

Combine sugar and water in small pan, stir over heat, without boiling, until sugar is dissolved. Simmer, uncovered, without stirring, about 10 minutes or until thickened slightly.

In a clean pan, combine wine, juice, jelly and spices, stir over heat until jelly dissolves; bring to boil. Strain into syrup, discard solids. Cool syrup. Pour mixture into lamington pan, cover; freeze until almost set.

Beat sorbet with egg white in large bowl with electric mixer, or process, until smooth. Pour into loaf pan, cover; freeze until firm.

cinnamon and vanilla ice-cream

1 vanilla bean

300ml cream

1³/₄ cups (430ml) milk

¹/₄ cup (55g) sugar

3 cinnamon sticks, broken

6 egg yolks

¹/₂ cup (110g) sugar, extra

Split vanilla bean, remove and reserve seeds. Combine vanilla bean and reserved seeds, cream, milk, sugar and cinnamon in medium pan, bring to boil. Remove from heat, cover, stand 30 minutes.

Beat egg yolks and extra sugar in small bowl with electric mixer until thick and creamy, gradually stir in milk mixture. Return mixture to same pan, cook, stirring, over low heat, without boiling, until mixture thickens slightly. Strain mixture, discard cinnamon and vanilla. Cover surface of custard with plastic wrap, cool to room temperature. Pour mixture into lamington pan, cover; freeze until almost set.

Chop ice-cream roughly, beat in large bowl with electric mixer, or process, until smooth. Pour into loaf pan, cover; freeze until firm.

fresh mint
ice-cream

1¹/₄ cups (275g) sugar

1¹/₄ cups (310ml) water

²/₃ cup fresh mint leaves

¹/₃ cup (80ml) lime juice

600ml thickened cream

Combine sugar and water in medium pan, stir over heat, without boiling, until sugar is dissolved. Simmer, uncovered, without stirring, 5 minutes. Cool slightly. Blend or process syrup with mint and juice until pureed. Push through coarse nylon sieve (to prevent mint discolouring); discard mint. Pour mixture into lamington pan, cover; freeze until almost set.

Chop ice-cream mixture roughly, beat in large bowl with electric mixer, or process, until smooth. Beat cream in small bowl with electric mixer until soft peaks form, fold into ice-cream mixture, in several batches. Pour mixture into lamington pan, cover; freeze until almost set.

Chop ice-cream roughly, beat in large bowl with electric mixer, or process, until smooth. Pour into loaf pan, cover; freeze until firm.

Serves 4 to 6

coconut
ice-cream

400ml can coconut cream

300ml cream

1 cup (250ml) milk

1 vanilla bean

6 egg yolks

$3/4$ cup (165g) sugar

$2/3$ cup (60g) desiccated coconut

Combine coconut cream, cream, milk and vanilla bean in large pan, bring to boil; remove vanilla bean. Whisk egg yolks and sugar in large bowl until combined. **Gradually** whisk hot milk mixture into yolk mixture, return to same pan, stir over low heat, without boiling, until mixture is thickened slightly; stir in coconut. Pour mixture into lamington pan, cover; freeze until almost set. **Chop** ice-cream roughly, beat in large bowl with electric mixer, or process, until smooth. Pour into loaf pan, cover; freeze until firm.

Serves 4 to 6

glossary

almonds
flaked: paper-thin slices.
kernels: natural kernels with skins.

amaretti biscuits small Italian-style macaroons based on ground almonds.

Amaretto almond-flavoured liqueur.

biscuits, plain sweet also known as cookies, an uniced plain biscuit such as Milk Coffee or Nice.

breadcrumbs, packaged fine-textured, crunchy, purchased, white breadcrumbs.

carambola also known as star fruit; five-cornered, pale golden-yellow, crisp and juicy fruit with a waxy edible skin.

cheese, mascarpone a fresh, thick, triple-cream cheese with a delicately sweet, slightly sour taste.

chestnut spread also known as sweetened chestnut puree or creme de marrons; made of pureed chestnuts, candied chestnut pieces, sugar, glucose syrup and vanilla. Available from good delicatessens; not to be confused with chestnut puree, made only of pureed chestnuts and water.

chocolate
bittersweet: good quality eating chocolate with a low sugar content. We used the Lindt brand.
dark eating chocolate: made of cocoa liquor, cocoa butter and sugar.

dark cooking: we used premium quality dark cooking chocolate rather than compound.
melts: available in milk, white and dark chocolate. Made of sugar, vegetable fats, milk solids, cocoa powder, butter oil and emulsifiers, these are good for melting and moulding.
white: eating chocolate.

chocolate hazelnut spread we used Nutella.

honeycomb bars/pieces chocolate-dipped honeycomb; made from chocolate, sugar, glucose and gelatine. We used Violet Crumble.

Ice Magic a commercial chocolate ice-cream coating that when poured onto ice-cream will form a crackly shell in seconds. Available from supermarkets.

coconut
cream: available in cans and cartons; made from coconut and water.
desiccated: unsweetened, concentrated, dried shredded coconut.
milk pure, unsweetened: coconut milk available in cans.

coconut macaroons small biscuits based on coconut.

Cointreau citrus-flavoured liqueur.

cornflour also known as cornstarch; used as a thickening agent in cooking.

cream
fresh: (minimum fat content 35%) also known as pure cream and pouring cream; has no additives like commercially thickened cream.
thickened: (minimum fat content 35%) a whipping cream containing a thickener.

custard powder packaged, vanilla pudding mixture.

essences also known as extracts; generally the byproduct of distillation of plants.

food colourings available in liquid, powdered and concentrated paste forms.

fruit mince mince meat.

fruity mallow bakes coloured marshmallow pellets; made from sugar, glucose, cornflour and gelatine.

gelatine (gelatin) we used powdered gelatine. It is also available in sheet form known as leaf gelatine.

ginger, fresh also known as green or root ginger, the thick gnarled root of a tropical plant. Can be kept, peeled, covered with dry sherry in a jar and refrigerated, or frozen in an airtight container.

golden sponge cake mix plain white cake mix.

Grand Marnier orange-flavoured liqueur based on cognac-brandy.

hazelnuts also known as filberts; plump, grape-size, rich, sweet nuts.

Irish whiskey the Irish were the first to make whiskey; theirs is a smooth, light, dry type made from distilled fermented barley.

Jersey caramels made from sugar, glucose, condensed milk, flour, oil and gelatine.

Kahlua coffee-flavoured liqueur.

kiwi fruit also known as Chinese gooseberry.

lamington pan a shallow (2.5cm deep) 20cm x30cm rectangular pan.

licorice toffees a commercially made licorice-flavoured caramel confection.

Malibu coconut-flavoured rum.

maple syrup distilled sap of the maple tree. Maple-flavoured syrup or pancake syrup is made from cane sugar and artificial maple flavouring and is not an adequate substitute for the real thing.

Maraschino a cherry-flavoured liqueur.

Midori a green, melon-flavoured liqueur.

milk we used full-cream homogenised milk unless otherwise specified.

evaporated unsweetened canned milk from which water has been extracted by evaporation.

evaporated light canned milk with 0.3 percent fat content.

sweetened condensed a canned milk product consisting of milk with more than half the water content removed and sugar added to the milk which remains.

persimmon (also known as the date plum) is thought to be a fruit native to China. The fruit must be very soft and ripe or it will have an astringent taste. Peel away skin before eating.

pink prickly pear also known as cactus pear. A sweet-flavoured fruit. Use rubber gloves when peeling and chopping.

redcurrant jelly a preserve made from redcurrants used as a glaze for desserts or in sauces.

rice, white short grain fat, almost round grain with a high starch content; tends to clump together when cooked.

rum made from fermented sugarcane.

dark: we prefer to use an underproof rum (not overproof) for a more subtle flavour.

white: we use Bacardi rum which is colourless.

Snickers Bars made from chocolate, peanuts, glucose, sugar, milk powder, butter and egg white.

sponge finger biscuits also known as savoiardi, savoy biscuits or ladyfingers. They are crisp and made from sponge-cake.

sugar we used coarse, granulated table sugar, also known as crystal sugar, unless otherwise specified.

brown: an extremely soft sugar retaining molasses for its characteristic colour and flavour.

caster: also known as superfine or finely granulated table sugar.

icing sugar mixture: also known as confectioners' sugar or powdered sugar; granulated sugar crushed together with a small amount (about 3%) cornflour added.

Tim Tams chocolate biscuits coated in chocolate.

vanilla bean dried long, thin pod from a tropical golden orchid grown in Central and South America and Tahiti; The minuscule black seeds inside the bean are used to impart a luscious vanilla flavour in baking and desserts.

vegetable oil any of a number of oils sourced from plants rather than animal fats.

watermelon large green-skinned melon with crisp juicy red flesh.

wooden hobby sticks we used Paddle Pop sticks available from craft shops.

yogurt plain unflavoured low-fat plain: we used yogurt with a fat content of less than 0.2 percent.

62

index

facts & figures

These conversions are approximate only, but the difference between an exact and the approximate conversion of various liquid and dry measures is minimal and will not affect your cooking results.

Note: NZ, Canada, US and UK all use 15ml tablespoons. Australian tablespoons measure 20ml. All cup and spoon measurements are level.

Measuring equipment
The difference between one country's measuring cups and another's is, at most, within a 2 or 3 teaspoon variance. (For the record, 1 Australian metric measuring cup holds approximately 250ml.) The most accurate way of measuring dry ingredients is to weigh them. For liquids, use a clear glass or plastic jug having metric markings.

How to measure
When using graduated measuring cups, shake dry ingredients loosely into the appropriate cup. Do not tap the cup on a bench or tightly pack the ingredients unless directed to do so. Level the top of measuring cups and measuring spoons with a knife. When measuring liquids, place a clear glass or plastic jug having metric markings on a flat surface to check accuracy at eye level.

Dry measures

metric	imperial
15g	½oz
30g	1oz
60g	2oz
90g	3oz
125g	4oz (¼lb)
155g	5oz
185g	6oz
220g	7oz
250g	8oz (½lb)
280g	9oz
315g	10oz
345g	11oz
375g	12oz (¾lb)
410g	13oz
440g	14oz
470g	15oz
500g	16oz (1lb)
750g	24oz (1½lb)
1kg	32oz (2lb)

We use large eggs with an average weight of 60g.

Liquid measures

metric	imperial
30 ml	1 fluid oz
60 ml	2 fluid oz
100 ml	3 fluid oz
125 ml	4 fluid oz
150 ml	5 fluid oz (¼ pint/1 gill)
190 ml	6 fluid oz
250 ml (1cup)	8 fluid oz
300 ml	10 fluid oz (½ pint)
500 ml	16 fluid oz
600 ml	20 fluid oz (1 pint)
1000 ml (1litre)	1¾ pints

Helpful measures

metric	imperial
3mm	⅛in
6mm	¼in
1cm	½in
2cm	¾in
2.5cm	1in
6cm	2½in
8cm	3in
20cm	8in
23cm	9in
25cm	10in
30cm	12in (1ft)

Oven temperatures
These oven temperatures are only a guide.
Always check the manufacturer's manual.

	°C (Celsius)	°F (Fahrenheit)	Gas Mark
Very slow	120	250	½
Slow	140 – 150	275 – 300	1 – 2
Moderately slow	170	325	3
Moderate	180 –190	350 – 375	4 – 5
Moderately hot	200	400	6
Hot	220 – 230	425 – 450	7 – 8
Very hot	240	475	9

at your fingertips

These elegant slipcovers store up to 10 mini books and make the books instantly accessible.

And the metric measuring cups and spoons make following our recipes a piece of cake.

Book Holder
Australia and overseas: $8.95 (incl. GST).

Metric Measuring Set
Australia: $6.50 (incl. GST).
New Zealand: $A8.00.
Elsewhere: $A9.95.
Prices include postage and handling. This offer is available in all countries.

Photocopy and complete coupon below

Mail or fax Photocopy and complete the coupon below and post to ACP Books Reader Offer, ACP Publishing, GPO Box 4967, Sydney NSW 2001, *or* fax to (02) 9267 4967.

Phone Have your credit card details ready, then phone 136 116 (Mon-Fri, 8.00am-6.00pm; Sat, 8.00am-6.00pm).

Australian residents We accept the credit cards listed on the coupon, money orders and cheques.

Overseas residents We accept the credit cards listed on the coupon, drafts in $A drawn on an Australian bank, and also British, New Zealand and U.S. cheques in the currency of the country of issue. Credit card charges are at the exchange rate current at the time of payment.

☐ **Book Holder** ☐ **Metric Measuring Set**
Please indicate number(s) required.

Mr/Mrs/Ms _____

Address _____

_____

Postcode _____ Country _____

Ph: Business hours ( ) _____

I enclose my cheque/money order for $ _____ payable to ACP Publishing.

OR: please charge $ _____ to my ☐ Bankcard ☐ Mastercard

☐ Visa ☐ American Express ☐ Diners Club

Expiry date ____ /____

| | | | | | | | | | | | | | | | | |

Card number

Cardholder's signature _____

Please allow up to 30 days delivery within Australia.
Allow up to 6 weeks for overseas deliveries.
Both offers expire 31/12/05. HLICE05

Food director Pamela Clark
Food editor Karen Hammial
Assistant food editor Kathy McGarry
Assistant recipe editor Elizabeth Hooper
ACP BOOKS
Editorial director Susan Tomnay
Creative director Hieu Chi Nguyen
Senior editor Julie Collard
Concept design Jackie Richards
Designer Jackie Richards
Design assistant Josii Do
Sales director Brian Cearnes
Publishing manager (rights & new projects) Jane Hazell
Brand manager Renée Crea
Sales & marketing coordinator Gabrielle Botto
Pre-press by Harry Palmer
Production manager Carol Currie
Chief executive officer John Alexander
Group publisher Pat Ingram
Publisher Sue Wannan
Editor-in-chief Deborah Thomas
Produced by ACP Books, Sydney.
Printing by Dai Nippon Printing in Korea.
Published by ACP Publishing Pty Limited, 54 Park St, Sydney;
GPO Box 4088, Sydney, NSW 2001.
Ph: (02) 9282 8618 Fax: (02) 9267 9438.
acpbooks@acp.com.au
www.acpbooks.com.au
To order books phone 136 116.
Send recipe enquiries to
Recipeenquiries@acp.com.au
Australia Distributed by Network Services, GPO Box 4088, Sydney, NSW 1028.
Ph: (02) 9282 8777 Fax: (02) 9264 3278.
United Kingdom Distributed by Australian Consolidated Press (UK), Moulton Park Busin. Centre, Red House Road, Moulton Park, Northampton, NN3 6AQ. Ph: (01604) 497 531 Fax: (01604) 497 533 acpukltd@aol.com
Canada Distributed by Whitecap Books Ltd, 351 Lynn Ave, North Vancouver, BC, V7J 2C4 Ph: (604) 980 9852 Fax: (604) 980 8197 customerservice@whitecap.ca
www.whitecap.ca
New Zealand Distributed by Netlink Distributi Company, Level 4, 23 Hargreaves St, College Hill, Auckland 1, Ph: (9) 302 7616.
South Africa Distributed by PSD Promotions, 30 Diesel Road, Isando, Gauteng, Johannes PO Box 1175, Isando, 1600, Gauteng, Johan Ph: (27 11) 392 6065/7 Fax: (27 11) 392 607 orders@psdprom.co.za

Clark, Pamela.
Icecreams and Sorbets.

Includes index.
ISBN 1 86396 150 X

1. Ice cream, ices, etc.
I Title: Australian Women's Weekly.

641.862

© ACP Publishing Pty Limited 1999
ABN 18 053 273 546

First published 1999. Reprinted 2004, 2005

Cover: Melon sorbet, page 39.
Back cover: at left, Strawberry ice-cream c page 52; at right, Blueberry lemon sorbet, ;

Stylist: Jane Collins
Photographer: Scott Cameron